Do-It-Yourself Decorating

Step-by-Step
Decorative Painting

Peter & Paula Knott

Meredith® Press

Des Moines, Iowa

Contents

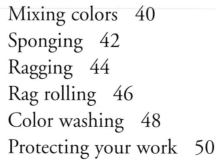

Introduction

This book has all the information you need to create both simple and more elaborate paint finishes in every room of your home.

In the "Ideas and Choices" chapter (page 6), we'll inspire you with the different finishes you can produce all through the house on just about any surface. You create most of these finishes with tools you have on hand, but in the "Tools and Materials" chapter (page 16), we'll show you a few tools you'll need for professional results and offer some handy alternatives. It's important to plan color schemes and carefully prepare your surfaces; in "Planning and Preparation" (page 26), we'll show you how.

Paint and water applied with a sponge or rag create stunning effects. These easy techniques are explained in "Simple Paint Effects" (page 38). Then you can advance to longer-drying glazes that give you more time to work on a surface for truly exciting results. We cover these in "Advanced Paint Finishes" (page 52).

Distressing techniques give you the softened look of age, as shown in "Antiquing and Faux Finishes" (page 74), where we also show you how easy it is to use paint to mimic expensive materials.

Even now, after years of using and teaching paint finishes, we're still coming up with new tips and shortcuts, many of which you'll find in this book. Have fun with the exciting paint finishes and special effects we'll help you create.

Ideas and Choices

With paint, you can achieve whatever look you're able to imagine. But paint's versatility also makes your choice of style, pattern, and color more difficult—there are so many from which to choose. This chapter features examples of rooms and furnishings that use painted finishes and effects to good advantage. Whether they're subtle or outrageous, they let you turn almost any surface into something special. Just be sure to carefully prepare your surfaces and give yourself time to practice and experiment with the finishes so you'll be proud of your results.

Ragged and color-washed effects

These paint effects use just small amounts of paint, together with common household items such as sponges and rags. The techniques are quick and easy as well as economical. Although very little skill is needed, you always should practice a finish on scrap material before starting your actual project. Single or multicolored washes create hazy, shaded effects, and ragged and rag-rolled finishes give you a wonderful marbled look. With both types, you'll find it easy to coordinate finish colors to blend with your furnishings.

► Blue color washing creates a sea and sky effect that's perfect for bathrooms.

▶ This sunny, multicolored wash befits an ultramodern teenager's bedroom. Color washing the radiator makes it blend in with the walls.

▼ A distinctive color wash in warm, earthy shades imparts age to bare plaster and makes a great backdrop for this modern sculpture.

◀ A pale cherry wash applied with vertical strokes creates an informal but stylish look that's ideal for a living room.

▼ Subtle rag rolling in two colors blends perfectly with this fawn background, creating just the right mood with just the right shades.

▶ It's easy to coordinate ragged walls with your furnishings. Just mix your colors for an exact match.

◀ Ragging in two colors over white walls helps to break up this large expanse with a marblelike texture.

Effects with bags and brushes

Water- or oil-based glazes can be blended together or partially removed from a surface. And you can use everything from plastic bags to toothbrushes to create unique textures with them. Dragging gives you a perfect border for other finishes, such as stippling and color washing, and multicolored bagging will amaze you with its ease and beauty. If an entire wall seems too large a project, don't worry. Just start with a smaller surface such as a door or piece of furniture.

▼ A highlight line rubbed into the moldings on these cupboards contrasts nicely with the subtle stippling and dragging.

▲ This mirror frame and closet are subtly dragged and stippled in a lemon-yellow glaze over a white background for a clean, fresh look.

▲ Bagging produces a wonderful texture on these cabinet doors—rich yet subtle.

◄ Complementary pink and green are stippled together on these closet doors to coordinate with the fabric print.

▲ These tongue-and-groove boards were dragged to highlight their vertical lines. Even the toilet seat was color-washed and varnished.

▲ This headboard was dragged and bagged to provide the right background for the stenciled image and to blend with the wall treatment.

Marble finishes

Paint effects that imitate stone and marble are always popular. Glazes give you time to blend colors, and their transparent quality helps them mimic the look of natural materials. Marble finishes take time, so carefully prepare your surfaces, and use a photo or an actual sample to help achieve realistic results. Break large areas into smaller ones so they'll be easier to work on. To create the effect of stone or marble blocks, use masking tape or stencils. Experiment with different veining techniques using feathers and brushes.

▼ Veining, created with both rags and brushes, produces a cool, marblelike effect.

▲ This marbled cornice (also shown at right) and baseboard provide an interesting frame for the patterned walls, as well as a nice juxtaposition of textures.

◀ These colors were carefully chosen and blended to coordinate with the walls.

◄ Two contrasting marbles used together can be dramatic. Here, they're highlighted by the dark chair rail and baseboard.

▼ This whimsical bagged look of marble—bold, dark, and finished with a gloss varnish—looks great below a chair rail.

◄ Newly painted marbled panels blend seamlessly with this antique slate fireplace.

▲ Stone finishes look especially good on stairs. Note the two contrasting treatments.

A variety of finishes

Call on paint effects for all sorts of applications—to create the illusion of age, to disguise a damaged surface, or just to create a great look. Wood graining works on any surface for natural and whimsical effects; crackle finishes give the impression of age on smaller items such as picture frames. You can transform a boring piece of furniture into a prized possession using a simple decorative paint finish. Best of all, once the base coat is on, all the hard work is done.

▲ The combination of light sponging above a chair rail and bolder rag rolling below works well in many rooms.

▼ Two colors were stippled together on these paneled doors, then accented with highlight lines around the molding.

◀ A waxed distressed finish of blue paint over a white base coat instantly ages this pine cabinet.

▼ The moldings and edges of this cabinet were distressed for an antique look.

▲ Color washes give wood a colorful, dramatic look and won't hide the grain as much as some other finishes.

Tools and Materials

Although you can create some wonderful painted finishes with ordinary paints and tools, sometimes you'll need special tools and materials to get the results you want. And in a few cases, using specialized professional tools and supplies is the only way to create a particular finish.

Basic tools

You've probably used—and already own—most of these common painting tools and supplies. But for any that you don't have, buy the best quality you can afford. Good tools used properly and taken care of will last for years. Also, keep painting staples such as sandpaper, steel wool, and rags on hand so you'll be ready to paint whenever the mood strikes you.

Stepladder
Traditional wooden stepladders have largely been replaced by lightweight aluminum designs. A ladder should be strong enough to remain completely stable under your weight. One that includes a platform is best.

Ladder
Single or extension ladders are especially handy for stairwells. Use them at an angle of about 70 degrees, and wrap the tops with soft cloth to avoid damaging the wall.

SAFETY NOTE
Make sure your ladder is stable and on an even surface before climbing it. Always reposition it as necessary.

Scaffold boards
Balance them on stepladders to make a platform that is good for working on high walls.

Drop cloths
Drop cloths or old bed sheets will protect furniture and floors and absorb spills.

Paintbrushes
Good-quality brushes in a variety of sizes are your most basic tools. Brushes that are cared for get better with age.

Short-nap roller
For applying oil or acrylic glazes to large, flat surfaces.

Sandpaper
Use medium- to fine-grit paper for preparation and between coats of varnish.

Level
Ensures accurate horizontal and vertical lines.

Chalk line
Makes a true vertical guideline for rag rolling. (A large key attached to chalk-coated string also works.)

Steel rule
For preparing large areas for marbling.

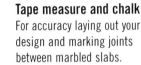

Masking tape
For protecting adjacent areas from paint.

Tape measure and chalk
For accuracy laying out your design and marking joints between marbled slabs.

Steel wool
Use medium- to fine-grade steel wool for distressing and applying wax to wood.

Old cotton towel
Removes glazes from brushes and other tools.

Screw-top glass jars with rubber seals
For mixing, shaking, and storing paint solutions.

Rags
For ragging, use clean polyester/cotton rags cut into 12-inch squares.

Stiff cardboard
A 12×8-inch piece makes a handy paint guard for protecting adjacent areas.

Old plate
Useful for holding small quantities of paint solution when sponging or color washing.

Plastic tubs
For holding paint or glaze when ragging or rag rolling. They make it easy to rewet the rag.

Special tools

Although you might get acceptable results with different or less expensive standard painting tools, there's really no substitute for the specialized brushes and equipment shown here. Buy the best brushes you can afford and clean them immediately after use with a solvent or soapy water (depending on the kind of paint you used), then hang them up to dry.

Flogger
Use large flogging brushes for large areas of dragging, simple graining, or color washing.

Distemper brush
Can be used in place of a flogger.

Mixed-bristle dragging brush
Produces a variety of lined effects. An ordinary long-bristled brush or a dust brush also will work.

Wallpaper brush
Used instead of a dragger or a flogger for washes.

Softening brushes
For blending and softening many finishes. Badger hair is the softest, but a dragging brush or a soft dust brush also will work.

Hog-hair softening brush

Badger-hair softening brush

Small dragging brush
Handy for detail work, such as the frame of a paneled door.

Dust brush
An alternative to a flogger or a dragging brush. Also used with softening brushes.

Stippling brushes
Available in a wide range of sizes and used to apply glaze finishes. Or, you can use plastic or rubber, textured plaster brushes or nylon block brushes. (Note: Oil glazes can eventually damage rubber.)

Nylon block brush
An economical alternative to a traditional stippling brush.

Alternative stippling brushes
Plastic or rubber, textured plaster brushes also can be used.

Sea sponge
Should have a good texture on both faces and, ideally, be unbleached. Choose one to fit your hand—about 5 inches in diameter.

Synthetic sponge
A cotton or synthetic sponge will work but may require shaping with scissors.

Rubber squeegee
Used for rubbing off a dark-colored glaze from the raised areas of a textured surface to expose a lighter-colored base.

Combs
Made of metal or rubber, these are ideal for wood-graining and other combed finishes.

Rockers
For producing a realistic open heartwood grain with either oil- or water-based glazes.

Feathers or fine artist's brush
Applies fine veins when marbling. The artist's brush also is used for touching up details in any fine work.

USING FEATHERS
Goose feathers are said to be the best for painting veins—the final step in creating marbling effects. Also, dipping a feather in solvent and lightly working it over the colored glaze will remove a little of the glaze and blur the edges to create a soft, veined effect.

Plastic grocery bags
Used to apply paint when bagging or marbling.

Bunch of keys
Beaten against a wooden surface, they mimic the knocks and bruises of age.

Brass-bristled brush
Removes soft grain from wooden surfaces prior to liming.

Paints and materials

Most paint finishes use a large volume of water mixed with a relatively small amount of strong-color water-based paints, water-based glazes, or in some cases oil-based paints or glazes. A few special effects require the special solutions shown here. In addition, some common decorating supplies come in handy.

Satin-finish oil-based paint
Ideal for hard-wear areas and as a base for glaze finishes.

Water-based paint
Suitable for general decorating, this paint also can be diluted for simple paint effects.

Stencil paint
Strong color choices make this quick-drying water-based paint ideal for simple paint effects or for tinting acrylic glazes.

Acrylic paint
Plastic, tough, resilient, and water-based, it's suitable for tinting acrylic glazes.

Artist's oils
Strong-pigment oil-based paint used for tinting oil-based glazes.

Artist's acrylics
Strong-pigmented water-based paint ideal for tinting acrylic glazes.

Universal stains
Strong-pigmented color tints for paint or glaze.

CAUTION

Because paints and glazes that contain solvents may cause irritation to the skin, always wear protective gloves.

Acrylic glaze

A water-based medium that may be tinted and used instead of oil glaze. It is unaffected by sun or heat but has a relatively short working time.

Oil glaze

Transparent oil-based medium for use as a transparent oil glaze. It can be tinted to match your color choices and has a long working time but yellows when exposed to sun and heat.

Gilt cream

Beeswax and turpentine wax with metal powder, used as a highlighter or to repair gilt surfaces.

Liming wax

Mixture of beeswax and titanium white powder used to lime open-grain wood.

Turpentine-based clear wax polish

Protects finishes on painted or wooden furniture; used to distress water-based paint.

Wax candle

Used to simulate worn areas when creating distressed effects. Wax is rubbed on selected areas only.

PAINT THINNER

A solvent for oil-based paints and glazes, thinner or mineral spirits are used for diluting oil-based paints and glazes to the proper consistency. In addition, most equipment used for applying oil-based solutions should be cleaned thoroughly with a solvent such as thinner or mineral spirits.

Petroleum jelly

Thick oil medium that doesn't set; used to distress wood.

PAINTS AND MATERIALS *(CONTINUED)*

Acrylic crackle glaze
Splits and crazes two layers of water-based or acrylic paint, below.

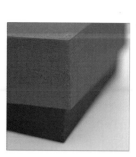

Acrylic crackle varnish
Produces surface cracks similar to those found in old varnish.

Patina varnish
Oil-based varnish that is used with gum arabic—also known as cracking varnish—to produce craquelure, or fine cracking similar to that on old porcelain or oil paintings.

Gum arabic
Used with patina varnish to produce craquelure, left. Craquelure creates a more delicate crazed effect than acrylic crackle glaze or acrylic crackle varnish, right.

Varnishes
Can be acrylic or oil-based and either sprayed or applied with a brush to protect the finish.

Emulsion glaze
Water-based protective medium, similar to varnish, that dries to a clear matte finish.

▲ **Acrylic varnish**

▶ **Oil-based varnish**

▲ **Spray varnish**

LIQUID DRIER
A medium that will reduce the drying time when mixed with oil-based paints and glazes.

PAINT MATERIALS AND THEIR USES

MATERIAL	SOLVENT	USE	ADVANTAGES	DISADVANTAGES	HAZARDS
WATER-BASED	Water	General decorating, Dilute for simple paint effects	Cheap and wide range of colors, Quick-drying	Not resistant to heavy wear	Minimal
ACRYLIC	Water	General decorating, For small items	Reasonable color range and durable, Quick-drying	Not widely available, Relatively expensive	Minimal
SOLVENT-BASED SATIN	Mineral Spirits	General decorating, For all surfaces	Widely available, Good color choice, Durable	Relatively expensive, Slow to dry	Avoid prolonged contact, Unpleasant smell
TRANSPARENT OIL GLAZE	Mineral Spirits	Suitable for decorative glazed finishes when tinted	Long working time, Easy to use	Tends to yellow, Long drying time	Avoid prolonged contact, Unpleasant smell
ACRYLIC GLAZE	Water	Suitable for decorative glazed finishes when tinted	Quick drying time, Non-yellowing	Short working time	Minimal but smell can be unpleasant
STENCIL PAINT	Water	Use as base paint or as tint for acrylic glaze	Good color choice, Quick-drying	Not widely available	Minimal
ARTIST'S OILS	Mineral Spirits	Use to tint oil glaze	Good color choice, Widely available, Concentrated pigments	Expensive, Can reduce drying time	Pigments can be toxic
UNIVERSAL STAINS	Mineral Spirits	Use to tint oil glaze	Widely available	Poor color choice	Pigments can be toxic
ACRYLIC VARNISH	Water	Protective medium used over water-based paints	No discoloration, Quick-drying	May cause staining over oil bases	Minimal
OIL VARNISH	Mineral Spirits	Protective medium, For any surface	Extremely durable, Widely available	Slow-drying, Tends to yellow	Avoid prolonged contact, Smell can be unpleasant
WATER-BASED GLAZE	Water	Protective medium	Quick-drying, Completely clear	Not very durable	Minimal
PATINA VARNISH	Mineral Spirits	Aging surfaces, Craquelure	Ideal for authentic look	Expensive	Avoid prolonged contact
GUM ARABIC	Water	Used with patina varnish to produce craquelure	Ideal for authentic look	Expensive, Can be resoftened, Requires protection	Avoid prolonged contact
ACRYLIC CRACKLE GLAZE	Water	Produces rough splitting of two water-based paints	Rapid and effective, but the finish will need care	Difficult to apply For small surfaces only	Minimal
ACRYLIC CRACKLE VARNISH	Water	Produces random cracking on water-based paints	Rapid and effective, but the finish will need care	Difficult to apply, For small surfaces only	Minimal
WAX	Turpentine	Wax finishing, Distressing	Good finish	Needs regular reapplication	Avoid prolonged contact

Planning and Preparation

Before applying any paint finish, it's important to plan your color scheme carefully. Select colors to coordinate with furnishings in the room and to complement the room's shape and decor, then create a number of different color samples. Attach your samples to the wall, floor, or whatever surface you're decorating, and look at them under both natural and artificial light. Then make your choice.

It's also essential to carefully prepare the surface you'll be decorating for the particular finish you'll apply. Some finishes will hide a poor surface, and others will highlight it. See the chart on pages 36–37 for more information.

Choosing colors

A basic understanding of how colors are mixed and how they interact is helpful. But the best way to guarantee a successful color scheme is to prepare a number of color samples and live with them for a few days in the room you're decorating. Your first color choice may not be the one you eventually pick.

MIXING COLORS

In theory, all colors are created from the three primary colors: blue, yellow, and red, together with black and white. The example at right, which blends together three glazes mixed with primary bases (see pages 52–55), shows how the primary colors blend and how difficult it is to get colors that are vibrant and true. But manufacturers now make so many colors that your mixing is limited to fine-tuning their premixed colors.

Using the color wheel

When combining colors for color schemes, there are three simple concepts to keep in mind for successful results.

Complementary colors

Colors on opposite sides of the color wheel are known as complementary colors because together they create a full complement of all the spectral hues. Each color is the other's strongest possible contrast. You've probably taken advantage of these color relationships, for example, when you wrapped an orange present in blue or purple tissue or gift wrap.

Analogous colors

Colors that appear next to each other on the color wheel are closely related and always blend well with each other. However, a scheme made up of only closely related colors won't have the zing that contrasts introduce.

Triadic schemes

Any three colors equidistant on the color wheel will harmonize with each other.

Reducing color strength

When two complementary colors are mixed, they produce a gray midtone. This can be useful when mixing colors. If a color is too vibrant, the addition of its complementary color will produce a less vibrant but still clean color. White reduces color strength to produce a tint while retaining its purity.

Color clarity is weakened by adding black.

Color value is reduced and made lighter by adding white.

Creating a balanced scheme

The intensity of a color is a measure of how dull or vivid it is; its value measures how dark or light it is. A balanced scheme is one in which no one color overpowers the others. It's as important to use colors of similar intensity and value as it is to coordinate them.

Mixed complementary colors produce gray midtones.

THE EFFECT OF LIGHT ON COLOR

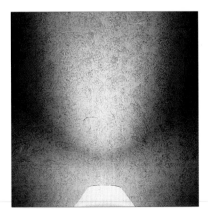

Artificial light

Light affects the appearance of colors. In yellowish artificial light, blue may appear green.

Natural light

It's important to check the colors you intend to use in both natural and artificial light.

COLOR COMBINATIONS

To come up with successful color schemes, make a note of the colors used in rooms that particularly appeal to you. Also, be aware of how color combinations work in nature. Always remember that a room's color scheme should act as a backdrop to your treasured possessions rather than overpower them.

Using color wisely

Choosing the right color scheme enhances and transforms a room, changing both its atmosphere and its apparent shape. Is the room light or dark, sunny or cold? Is it long and narrow or small but high-ceilinged? How do you use it? Take all these factors into account when you make your color choices. Look for all of the ways color might improve the room as a whole; don't just choose your favorite colors. You could get lucky and pick just the right colors by chance, but in the long run, it's better if you plan them according to established precepts.

CHOOSING THE STYLE

The versatility and ease with which you can choose colors, styles, and textures give paint finishes an advantage over other forms of decorating. But this very flexibility also is a source of frustration if you find that you don't know where to begin.

As a start, some key decorating principles are shown in the drawings on this page and page 31. The diagrams show the effect that dark and light, and warm and cold colors have on a room, and also how patterns of different kinds affect the apparent shape and size of a room. Color and pattern create illusions of more or less space than is actually there.

The first stage of planning a color scheme for an entire room—even before you begin to test color samples as described on page 28—is one you can do on paper. Take a photograph of the room you plan to decorate, then make several photocopies. Coloring in the photocopies in your alternate color schemes will point out any problems and help you decide which scheme works best.

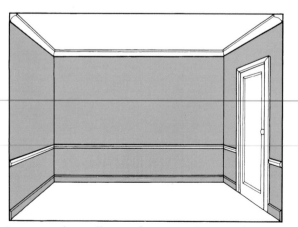

A warm color pulls a surface toward you and creates a cozy look.

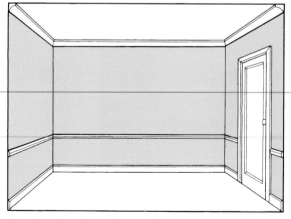

A cool color draws the surface away from you and creates an impression of space.

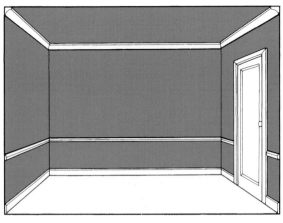

A dark color also draws a surface toward you and makes the ceiling appear lower.

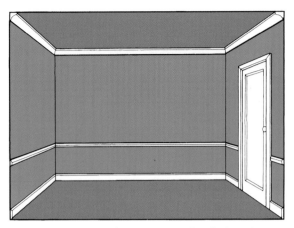

Using both a dark floor color and a dark ceiling color draws the two surfaces together.

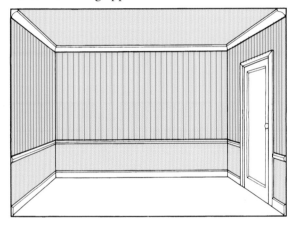

Vertical stripes pull the eye upward and appear to heighten a room.

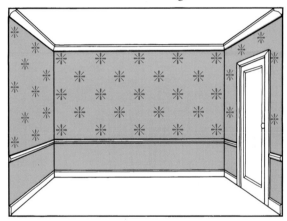

Large patterns bring walls toward you, making a room feel either claustrophobic or cozy.

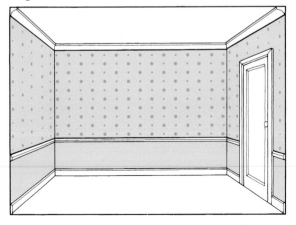

Small patterns, like cool colors, create an illusion of greater space.

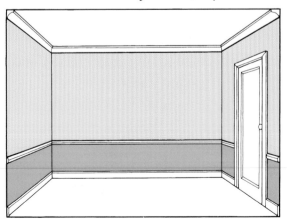

A darker color on the lower walls encloses the space; a light area above creates an illusion of space.

Preparing plaster surfaces

As always, the key to good painting results is careful preparation of surfaces. Not all surfaces need to be perfect—they just need to be appropriate for the finish you'll apply. Check the smoothness of a wall finish by rubbing your hand over it. A rough or textured surface isn't a good candidate for dragging, but you could sponge or rag it. The chart on pages 36–37 describes the ideal surface for each kind of paint finish. Refer to a general home improvement book if you need more information on preparing specific surfaces.

PLASTER SURFACES

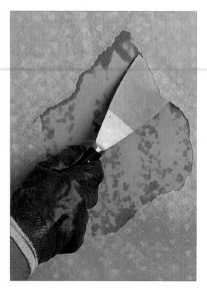  

1 First use a scraper to remove wallpaper or loose and flaking paint and plaster, then lightly sand the surface. Protect your hands with gloves, and wear a mask while working to make sure you don't inhale harmful sanding dust.

2 Clean the surface with a solution of liquid detergent or an all-purpose cleaner. Use a commercially available filler to repair any holes, filling them slightly higher than the wall surface to allow for shrinkage as the filler dries.

3 Sand the area when the filler has dried. Between the wood and walls, apply a flexible filler to conceal any gaps, then remove the excess filler with a damp sponge or rag.

4 Apply the base coat using a brush, roller, or pad. You'll need to use at least two coats. Lightly sand the surface between coats. Always follow the manufacturer's instructions, and take precautions against possible health hazards with the appropriate masks, gloves, and the recommended ventilation.

PROBLEMS AND SOLUTIONS

Concealing poor surfaces
Rag rolling in two colors (see pages 46–47) is not only quick, economical, and easy, but it's also an ideal finish for disguising walls that have especially poor or uneven surfaces.

Careful lighting
Lighting that pools across a wall will draw attention to any imperfections. Avoid highlighting surfaces you know are poor, even if you've used a paint finish to help disguise them.

Heavy-weight papers
Carefully remove heavy wall coverings. They can be difficult to strip, and if there's a poor surface beneath them, it may crumble. Heavy sponging with two or more colors (see pages 42–43) helps conceal or disguise such surfaces.

CAUTION
Always follow the manufacturer's instructions, particularly when using any products that contain solvents.

REPAIRING OLD PLASTER
Scrape off loose plaster and brush latex bonding agent over area. Apply patching plaster with putty knife; let dry. For deep holes, repeat.

Preparing wood surfaces

Wood furniture and accessories are especially good candidates for glaze finishes (see pages 52–73) and for antiquing and faux finishes (see pages 74–91). However, thorough surface preparation is essential for good results. All modern wood surfaces, from medium-density fiberboard (MDF) to melamine-finished chipboard, can be sanded and prepared for just about any kind of decorative finish. Refer to a good general home improvement book for more specific information. The chart on pages 36–37 lists the base coats you'll need for the finishes explained in this book.

WOOD AND WOOD-SUBSTITUTE SURFACES

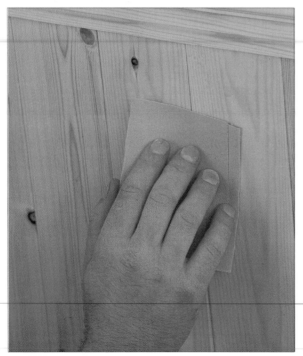

1 Prepare surfaces by lightly sanding to smooth rough edges and provide "tooth" for the paint. On painted surfaces or melamine, first clean with a detergent solution or all-purpose cleaner. Follow the instructions in Step 2 before applying the finish.

2 Remove all dust, first with a dust brush then with a lint-free rag dampened with alcohol. Seal any knots with shellac or an appropriate sealer. A tack cloth will remove any remaining dust and leave you with a completely clean surface.

3 Most paints are best applied in several thin coats rather than in one or two heavy ones. Before painting, be sure to coat bare wood surfaces with a primer then an undercoat.

4 Smooth the surface with fine-grit sandpaper before starting and between coats. Usually, furniture and built-ins, such as kitchen and bathroom cabinets, are painted with oil-based paints because they're considered more durable.

5 When applying paint finishes, choose the most appropriate base for the finish you're using (see pages 36–37). If necessary, apply a final coat of varnish to protect a water-based or oil-based paint finish from hard wear.

USING MEDIUM DENSITY FIBERBOARD
Although most traditional softwoods and hardwoods provide excellent surfaces for paint finishes, modern MDF is really the ideal surface. Be careful, though, when preparing an MDF surface—the sanding dust it produces is toxic. Wear a mask and work outside or indoors in a well-ventilated area.

CAUTION
Always follow the manufacturer's instructions, particularly when using any products that contain solvents.

CHOOSING PAINTS

FINISH	SPONGING	RAGGING	RAG ROLLING (WATER)	COLOR WASHING (SIMPLE)	RAGGING	RAG ROLLING (GLAZE)	STIPPLING	BAGGING	COLOR WASHING (ADVANCED)
PAGE NO.	42	44	46	48	56	58	60	64	68
DIFFICULTY (1–10, Easy–Hard)	1	1	2	2	2	3	2	2	3
IDEAL BASE	Flat water-based paint	Flat water-based paint	Flat water-based paint	Flat water-based paint	Satin paint	Satin paint	Satin paint	Satin paint	Satin paint
OTHER SUITABLE BASES	Semigloss water-based	Semigloss water-based	Semigloss water-based	Semigloss water-based	Semigloss water-based, Varnish, Melamine	Semigloss water-based, Varnish, Melamine	Semigloss water-based, Varnish, Melamine	Semigloss water-based, Varnish, Melamine	Semigloss water-based, Varnish, Melamine
BASE SURFACE	Possible on rough/poor surfaces	Possible on rough/poor surfaces	Possible on rough/poor surfaces	Possible on rough/poor surfaces	Good and smooth surface required	Any surface	Any surface	Any surface	Highlights imperfections
PAINT FINISH MEDIUM	Water-based paint solutions	Water-based paint solutions	Water-based paint solutions	Water-based paint solutions	Oil or acrylic glaze	Oil or acrylic glaze	Oil or acrylic glaze	Oil or acrylic glaze	Oil or acrylic glaze
PROTECTION RECOMMENDED	None	None	None	None	Suitable varnish	Suitable varnish	Suitable varnish	Suitable varnish	Suitable varnish
SUITABLE SURFACES	Walls or furniture	Walls or furniture	Walls or furniture	Walls or furniture	Walls or furniture	Walls or furniture	Walls or furniture	Walls or furniture	Walls or furniture
TOXICITY AND HAZARDS	Safe	Safe	Safe	Safe	Avoid prolonged skin contact with oil glaze, Dispose of waste safely	Avoid prolonged skin contact with oil glaze, Dispose of waste safely	Avoid prolonged skin contact with oil glaze, Dispose of waste safely	Avoid prolonged skin contact with oil glaze, Dispose of waste safely	Avoid prolonged skin contact with oil glaze, Dispose of waste safely

COLOR RUBBING	COMBING	DISTRESSING	WAX AGING	ACRYLIC CRACKLE	CRAQUELURE	LIMING	MARBLING	WOOD GRAINING (COMBS)	WOOD GRAINING (ROCKERS)
70	72	76	78	80	82	84	86	90	90
2	3	4	3	7	6	3	8	7	5
Satin paint	Satin paint	Any	Flat water-based paint	Water-based or acrylic	Satin paint	Open-grain wood	Satin paint	Satin paint	Satin paint
High-gloss water-based, Varnish Melamine	High-gloss water-based, Varnish Melamine	None	None	None	Any sealed surface	None	High-gloss water-based, Varnish, Melamine	High-gloss water-based, Varnish, Melamine	High-gloss water-based, Varnish, Melamine
Highlights imperfections	Good surface required	Highlights imperfections	Highlights imperfections	Highlights imperfections	Any surface	Any surface	Good surface required	Good surface required	Good surface required
Oil or acrylic glaze	Oil or acrylic glaze	Petroleum jelly or wax	Turpentine-based furniture wax	Acrylic crackle glaze/ varnish	Patina varnish and gum arabic	Liming wax	Oil or acrylic glaze	Oil or acrylic glaze	Oil or acrylic glaze
Suitable varnish	Suitable varnish	Suitable varnish	None	Varnish	Oil-based varnish	Furniture wax	Suitable varnish	Suitable varnish	Suitable varnish
Textured surfaces	Walls or furniture	Furniture	Furniture or wood paneling	Small, simple furniture	Any small surface	Any open-grain wood	Walls or furniture	Walls or furniture	Walls or furniture
Avoid prolonged skin contact with oil glaze, Dispose of waste safely	Avoid prolonged skin contact with oil glaze, Dispose of waste safely	Avoid prolonged skin contact with turpentine-based waxes	Avoid prolonged skin contact with turpentine-based waxes	Safe	Avoid prolonged contact with patina varnish	Avoid prolonged contact with wax containing turpentine and titanium	Avoid prolonged skin contact with oil glaze, Dispose of waste safely	Avoid prolonged skin contact with oil glaze, Dispose of waste safely	Avoid prolonged skin contact with oil glaze, Dispose of waste safely

Simple Paint Effects

For flexibility, style, speed, and affordability, it's hard to beat these simple paint effects. Some are traditional, adapted from more complicated glaze finishes (see pages 52–73); others are new effects that have been made possible by the kinds of paint now available. You'll be amazed at how easy it is to master such an ideal decorating medium—one that gives you control over color and pattern for a finish that's as individual as you are. Once you've mastered one of these paint effects, we predict you'll be so pleased with your results that you'll want to try them all.

Mixing colors

All paint effects are easier to accomplish with careful planning and surface preparation. Always practice on scrap material first to perfect your technique and to check your color scheme under both natural and artificial light. Paint solutions use surprisingly small quantities of strong-color paint mixed with comparatively large amounts of water, providing inexpensive but stunning results. A small glass jar containing just 1 tablespoon of paint and half-filled with water is enough to sponge two medium-size rooms.

MATERIALS: Strong-color paint (stencil, water-based, or acrylic paint), screw-top glass jar with a rubber seal, liquid measuring cup, absorbent towel or cloth

TYPICAL DILUTIONS AND COVERAGE FOR WATER–BASED FINISHES

	WATER : PAINT*	COVERAGE
SPONGING	10/30 : 1 (strong/pale)	less than ½ tsp. per square yard
RAGGING OR RAG ROLLING	5/25 : 1 (strong/pale)	1 tsp. per square yard
COLOR WASHING	10/20 : 1 (strong/pale)	1 Tbsp. per square yard

*Stencil paint or strong-color water-based paint

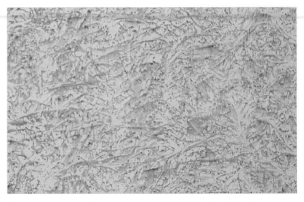

For strong colors, use a 5/10 : 1 dilution.

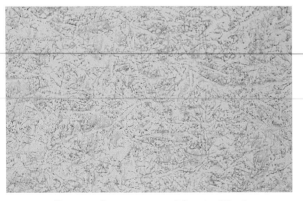

For medium colors, use a 20 : 1 dilution.

For weak colors, use a 30 : 1 dilution.

1 Prepare a work area with all of your supplies. Pour a small amount of paint into the screw-top jar.

2 Use a liquid measuring cup to add warm water in the right proportions for the paint effect (see the chart on page 40).

3 Replace the jar lid, cover the jar with an absorbent towel or cloth, and shake well.

4 Check the bottom of the jar to make sure the paint is completely mixed. If you don't, the color might vary during application. Shake again if necessary. Make a small sample of your finish on scrap paper to check both the finish and the color before you start work on the actual surface.

DECORATOR'S TIPS

Warm water helps dissolve the paint more quickly.

It's important to use the same intensity of all colors when using two or more different colors together.

Once mixed, the paint-and-water solution should last almost indefinitely if protected from freezing.

Sponging

Sponging is one of the quickest and cheapest ways to decorate and coordinate a room. It's fun to apply to walls, furniture, and accessories and, depending on the colors you use and the way you hold the sponge, it gives you a background that's soft and subtle or bold and outrageous. Sponging also hides some wall flaws and even will disguise poor plaster and textured wall coverings (see page 33). Mistakes are easy to correct, too: Simply sponge on a little undiluted base-coat paint with a clean sponge.

TOOLS: Natural sea sponge, strip of cardboard

MATERIALS: Drop cloth, paint solutions in 2 or 3 colors, old plate, absorbent towel or cloth

BASE: Sponge over a base coat of water-based paint.

1 On a work surface protected by a drop cloth, pour out 1 Tbsp. of paint solution (see pages 40–41). Mop it up with the sponge so the paint is evenly distributed across the sponge's surface.

2 Test the paint coverage on scrap paper first. Then apply the sponge to the wall with a gentle patting motion, rotating your hand and sponge as you work to achieve an even but somewhat random distribution of color.

3 To sponge close to the ceiling or into corners, use a strip of stiff, thin cardboard to protect the adjacent wall. Use the cloth to wipe up any spills.

4 A paint-loaded sponge will cover about 7–14 square yards before it requires reloading. For a dense texture, go around the room several times, gradually building up the color.

5 You can always add more color, but it's often hard to remove excess color. Check the area often by standing back to look at the overall effect. Stop sponging when you achieve the desired look.

6 Additional colors can be added right away, since the paint dries in about a minute. You can use the same sponge for applying the other colors, but you'll need to wash and dry it between color changes.

7 To coordinate the finish with a room's furnishings, pick colors that already appear in the room's decor. In this case, green was used for the first coat, followed by pink and peach.

DENSITY OF SPONGING

Dense sponging
This produces a bold, dramatic finish, with shapes that blend into an overall pattern.

Light sponging
With lots of space to let the base-coat color show through, this produces a soft, airy finish.

PREPARATION
Always prepare samples before you start on the actual surface to be decorated. Your natural sea sponge should be comfortable to hold and have an open texture on both the front and back surfaces.

Dry sponges expand when wet, so choose one that's slightly smaller than hand-size when it's dry. Then it should fit nicely into your hand when it's wet.

A synthetic sponge can be used but it won't produce the same interesting pattern.

Ragging

Ragging with a water-based paint solution is a simple variation on traditional sponging. You can choose between a strong, dramatic effect or a soft, subtle look with a texture similar to crushed velvet. Always make a sample to check colors and the finish before you start on the actual surface.

TOOLS: Prewashed polyester-cotton (or 100% cotton) rags without hems, about 12 inches square; strip of thin cardboard

MATERIALS: Drop cloth, water-based paint solutions in 1 to 3 colors, plastic tub, cloth

BASE: On walls, rag over a base coat of water-based paint.

1 On a work surface protected by a drop cloth, transfer paint solution (see pages 40–41) to a plastic container. Take a rag and immerse it in the paint solution.

2 Squeeze out the rag over the tub, catching any drips on the tub edge with the outside of your hand. Any excess paint on your hands will be absorbed by the fabric.

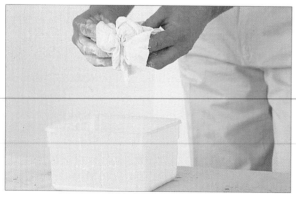

3 Scrunch the rag into a manageable-size ball. Don't try to fold it; this will leave hard lines on the finished effect.

4 Apply the rag to the wall using a gentle, patting motion. Build up the color in a random pattern until you achieve the desired density.

5 At the corners and tops of walls, use the cardboard to protect the adjacent wall from paint smudges. Apply the rag close to the corner. Repeat when you start on the next wall.

REWETTING THE RAG

After covering about 1 square yard, the rag will start to dry out. Rewet it by dipping your hand into the paint solution and wiping it over the rag. Do this twice.

6 Add a second color on a clean rag, using the same procedure. You can follow with two or three more colors, adding them all at once or applying them one layer at a time.

7 To correct a mistake, sponge on some undiluted base-coat paint. If this destroys some of the ragging, repeat the ragging over those areas.

SUBTLE FINISHES
Ragging is especially effective combined with sponging (see pages 42–43) and color washing (see pages 48–49).

USE YOUR BARE HANDS
Don't try wearing rubber gloves for ragging. They're clumsy and can ruin the delicate ragging effect.

STORING SURPLUS PAINT
You can store the rag in the same jar with the leftover paint solution so you'll have both handy for touch-ups and repairs.

Light ragging
Light ragging in blue and brown on a dove-gray background.

Blue-and-brown ragging
Both colors applied on a medium-green background.

Rag rolling

Rag rolling using a water-based paint solution is easier than rag rolling with glazes (see pages 58–59), which is more time-consuming and almost always a lot messier. It produces a wonderful "crinkled" pattern that, like sponging and ragging, will hide poorly textured wall surfaces.

TOOLS: Prewashed polyester-cotton (or 100% cotton) rags without hems, about 12 inches square; plumb line; strip of thin cardboard

MATERIALS: Drop cloth, water-based paint solutions in 1 to 3 colors, plastic tub, cloth

BASE: On walls, rag-roll over a base coat of water-based paint.

1 Pour the paint solution (see pages 40–41) into the container on a protected work surface, and immerse a rag in it.

2 Squeeze out the rag over the tub, wiping the outside of your hand on the edge of the tub to catch any drips. Any excess paint on your hands will be absorbed by the fabric.

3 Scrunch the rag into a sausage shape—don't try to neatly fold or roll it. Each time the rag is rewetted with paint, it will need to be rescrunched to avoid making a repetitive pattern on the wall.

4 Use both hands to roll the rag up the wall in a straight, vertical column about 4 inches wide. Use a plumb line as a guide for the first line. When the column is complete, remove the rag.

5 Stop the columns where you can comfortably reach in one stretch, but stagger the tops. Split the wall horizontally into three sections, then do each one separately.

6 After about 1 square yard, the rag will start to dry out. To rewet the rag, dip your hand into the solution and wipe it on the rag. Repeat once more. This will let you cover another square yard.

7 Use the ragging technique (see pages 44–45) in a vertical line at the corners. Place the cardboard strip against the adjacent wall to protect it.

8 You can apply second and third colors over the first to create columns of mixed colors on top of each other, or stripes of different colors side by side.

THE EFFECT OF ONE OR MORE COLORS

A luxurious three-color blend

Ragging in a single cool color

Ragging in a single warm color

DESIGN IDEA

Rag-rolling a wall can give you a sophisticated look, especially when you use extra colors. Try it with three colors up to a chair rail, then use sponging or ragging on the wall above the rail.

Color washing

Color washing with water-based paint solutions produces finishes that range from subtle clouding to a wild, shimmering underwater look. Although it draws attention to rough wall surfaces, this may be an advantage if you're planning a distressed look.

TOOLS: Absorbent cloth, synthetic sponge

MATERIALS: Drop cloth, water-based paint solution, old plate

BASE: On walls, color-wash over a base coat of water-based paint. On woodwork, use a base coat of satin paint.

COLOR-WASH TECHNIQUES

For walls, choose from circular shapes, a random "hay bundle" pattern, or horizontal or vertical stripes.

Move the sponge over the surface in a random circular or figure-eight motion. Create the hay-bundle pattern by covering the surface with arcs of long, overlapping strokes. Make the stripes with short overlapping strokes.

New wood will absorb paint evenly. But if the wood has been painted and stripped, it may be difficult to get an even finish; always make a test sample first. Varnish or wax color-washed furniture to protect it.

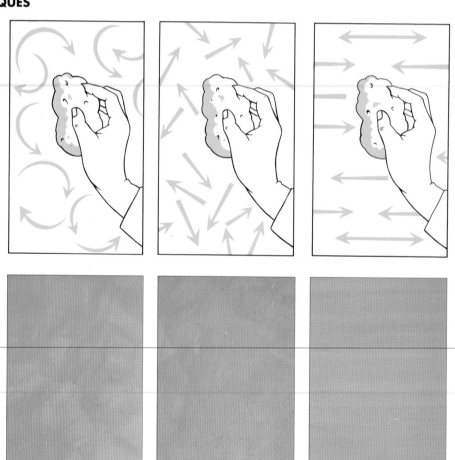

Circular shapes

Random patterns

Horizontal or vertical stripes

1 On a work surface protected by a drop cloth, pour about 1 Tbsp. of paint solution (see pages 40–41) onto a plate and work it into the sponge. Practice your technique on scrap material before color-washing the actual surface because both color and pattern can vary. Also, try out any pattern (see page 48) and color alternatives before deciding on the color and effect you prefer.

2 Using your chosen color, apply the sponge to the well-prepared and evenly painted wall, using the technique you've chosen. Work quickly and rewet the sponge when necessary—probably about every 1 square yard. Use a small brush to get into awkward corners. You can add additional colors, but give the paint about an hour to dry between coats.

COLOR–WASH EFFECTS ON WOOD AND PLASTER

◀ **One-color wash**
Choose a light or medium-tone background, and wash in a slightly deeper tone. These orange shades blend for a warm and subtle effect.

▶ **Two-color wash**
Contrasting colors can be washed over each other.

◀ **On new wood**
Color washing emphasizes the grain and gives wood a subtle aged look.

KEEP UP THE GOOD WORK
Work quickly when color washing, and try to maintain a wet edge. Always complete an entire wall at a time.

Protecting your work

On walls, simple paint effects are good at hiding lumps, bumps, and scuff marks, and they don't usually need further protection to weather reasonable wear and tear. Most water-based paints can be wiped clean, but certain areas that are especially prone to scuffs, such as hallways, kitchens, and bathrooms, as well as furniture and woodwork, will benefit from some kind of protective finish.

If you use a gloss finish, expect it to highlight all surface imperfections; flat and satin finishes usually are more forgiving. However, some paint effects—such as color washing in rich, dark colors—are enhanced by gloss varnish, so the shinier, the better.

TOOLS: Paintbrush, fine-grit sandpaper, fine-grade steel wool

MATERIALS: Varnish or other protective finish (see page 25)

▲ FLAT, SEMIGLOSS, AND GLOSS FINISHES

A flat finish leaves the color unchanged; semigloss and gloss finishes enrich and deepen the color and create highlights.

◄ OIL-BASED VARNISH

This is available in flat, satin, and gloss finishes and may contain polyurethane, which makes it tough and heat-resistant. Oil-based varnish contains linseed oil, which has a slight yellowing effect that becomes stronger with age and can change the tones of blues and reds. Use over oil glazes, especially if the item will get heavy wear. Brush on two or three coats, sanding lightly between each one.

SPRAY VARNISH

Varnish is oil- or water-based and is ideal for protecting small, ornate items. Use several thin coats rather that one thick coat. Follow the manufacturer's instructions when applying, and use fine steel wool to give the varnish tooth between coats.

CAUTION

Carefully follow the manufacturer's instructions and safety precautions, especially when working with products that contain solvents. Always work in a well-ventilated space, and wear gloves and protective clothing to prevent contact with your skin.

ACRYLIC VARNISH

This is the best varnish for protecting water-based finishes that are exposed to wear, from furniture to woodwork. It comes in matte, satin, and gloss finishes. Apply it with a brush or spray (for small objects). It has a milky color during application but dries clear. Use two or three coats, sanding lightly between each.

PROTECTIVE GLAZE

This water-based glaze is similar to acrylic varnish. Apply it by brush or spray for an invisible protective layer, although one that's not quite as durable as some of the other finishes discussed above.

Check the manufacturer's instructions to make sure the glaze is compatible with the base coat of the finish you've applied.

CHANGING THE EFFECT

Always add the protective finish to your test samples, too; varnish changes the final color.

Advanced Paint Finishes

The flexibility you get from glazes opens up opportunities for a whole new array of exciting paint effects. Because glazes take more time to dry, they give you more time to work with them to produce a fine finish. They also let you blend more than one glaze and let you work them together on the surface at the same time. This produces effects that have a special depth and quality.

Because acrylic and oil glazes aren't especially tough finishes, when you use them on surfaces such as doors, floors, and furniture, they'll need a coat of sealer or varnish if they're going to wear well. The varnish you choose must be compatible with the glaze used or you could end up damaging your masterpiece. Use the varnish recommended by the glaze manufacturer (see pages 22–23 and 50–51).

This chapter contains

Mixing glazes

Acrylic glazes are nontoxic, tough, nonyellowing, and water-based. They can be applied over water-based semigloss paint, satin paint, or melamine. Oil glaze contains linseed oil and gives high-quality results, but it yellows with age and when exposed to high temperatures or bright light. It can be used over satin paint or on top of a melamine base.

Acrylic glaze
TOOLS: Small paintbrush or spoon

MATERIALS: Drop cloth, stencil paint, artist's acrylic paint or universal stain, screw-top glass jar with rubber seal, acrylic glaze, absorbent cloth

Oil glaze
TOOLS: Small paintbrush or spoon

MATERIALS: Drop cloth, artist's oils, semigloss paint or universal stain, transparent oil glaze, screw-top glass jar with rubber seal, thinner or turpentine, absorbent cloth

RELATIVE QUANTITIES OF COLOR AND GLAZE TO SOLVENT

Acrylic glaze
- 15–20% Water
- 75–80% Acrylic glaze
- 5% Colorant

Oil-based glaze
- 15% Alcohol or turpentine
- 80% Oil glaze
- 5% Artist's oil

USING GLAZES

	ACRYLIC	OIL
MAXIMUM WORKING TIME	30 minutes	90 minutes
DRYING TIME	2–4 hours	8–16 hours
COVERAGE	12–25 square yards per pint	12–25 square yards per pint
SUITABLE SURFACES	Water-based semigloss	Oil-based satin
	Oil–based satin	Melamine
	Melamine	Varnished surfaces
	Varnished surfaces	
SUITABLE COLORANTS	Stencil or acrylic paints	Artist's oils, satin
	Universal stain	Universal stain
COMMENTS	Water-based—dries clear	Easy to use but yellows with age

ACRYLIC GLAZE

1 Protect the work surface and pour 1 Tbsp. of the paint (in this case, stencil paint) into the jar. (If you use artist's acrylic, add a little water and use a brush or a spoon to mix it.) Add water and the glaze, using the proportions shown in the chart on page 54.

2 For a soft color, use about one part paint or stain to 20 parts glaze; for a strong effect, use about one part paint or stain to 10 parts glaze. Replace the jar lid, cover the jar with a piece of cloth, and shake vigorously to thoroughly mix.

3 Check the bottom of the jar to make sure the paint is thoroughly mixed. If it's not, shake again. Check the glaze for color intensity and consistency by making a sample. Let dry. If the color is too strong or too pale, adjust and test again.

OIL-BASED GLAZE

1 Protect the work surface with the drop cloth. Squeeze about a 2-inch length of artist's oil paint into the resealable jar. Because you will thin this paint, use a color darker than the desired final color. If you use satin paint or universal stain, use about 2 Tbsp. of artist's paint.

2 Add about 1 fl. oz. or ½-inch depth of thinner or turpentine. Mix the paint and solvent with a brush or spoon. Add about 5 fl. oz. or 2 inches of glaze. Don't use more than 20 percent solvent in the mixture (it will over-thin the glaze). Seal the jar, cover it well, and shake.

3 Check the bottom of the jar for any lumps in the mixture. Continue to shake the jar if the ingredients aren't thoroughly mixed. This is especially important when using artist's oils because the undissolved paint creates a glaze that changes color during use.

Dragging

Dragging is a subtle finish that works well on large areas such as walls and provides a soft, striped effect on doors, woodwork, and paneling. When the first color is dry, you can add more colors for extra interest. Mixed-bristle dragging brushes will give you a more defined line, similar to combing (see pages 72–73).

TOOLS: 1-inch paintbrush, brush for dragging (see box, page 57)

MATERIALS: Drop cloth, mixed glaze in 1 color (see pages 54–55), old towel or absorbent cloth

BASE: This finish can be used over almost any solid-colored surface painted with semigloss paint (see pages 36–37).

1 Prepare the surface (see pages 32–37). Dragging tends to highlight any wall imperfections. Protect the work area with the drop cloth, and transfer the glaze into a container.

2 Apply the mixed glaze using an appropriate-size paintbrush. Spread it evenly over the surface.

3 Starting from a top corner, draw the brush down through the glaze in vertical lines, holding it at about a 30-degree angle to the wall. Continue the stroke as far as you can to avoid making too many joints.

4 If you want more defined lines, apply greater pressure to the brush as you make your strokes. As you work, occasionally pull the dragging brush through the towel to help keep it uniformly dry.

5 A brush leaves a mark when first applied to a surface but not when taken off. To disguise joints in the dragging, work back over previous areas, starting from a bottom corner and dragging from the opposite direction. This way, only the corners will show brush marks.

6 The result is a subtle grained effect, which highlights other aspects of the room without overpowering them.

BRUSH UP ON YOUR EQUIPMENT

To ensure consistent results, slightly dampen your brush with glaze before starting work; a damp brush creates a slightly different look than a dry one. If you don't have traditional dragging or flogging brushes, you can use any long-bristled paintbrush, a dust brush, a distemper brush, or a wallpaper-hanging brush.

Large areas of glaze go on more quickly using a short-nap roller instead of a brush.

SHARP DRAGGED CORNERS

The frame of a paneled door is an ideal surface for a dragged finish.

First complete the horizontal rails at the top and bottom of the door, then start work on the verticals from the door edges to create clean, sharp joints at the horizontal rails.

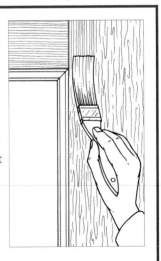

Rag rolling

Rag rolling with glaze produces a depth and quality of finish that would be difficult to achieve any other way. Compare this variation on traditional rag rolling, which uses only dry rags, with the rag rolling with water-based paint on pages 46–47. There's no reason why you can't combine the two for a truly special finish.

TOOLS: 1-inch paintbrush, prewashed polyester-cotton or 100% cotton rag about 12 inches square

MATERIALS: Drop cloth, plastic tub, mixed glaze in 1 color (see pages 54–55), thin rubber gloves, old towel or absorbent cloth

BASE: This finish can be used over a good-condition, solid-colored surface painted with satin paint (see pages 36–37).

1 Cover the work surface with the drop cloth. Transfer the mixed glaze (see pages 54–55) to the plastic tub, and immerse the rag in it.

2 Apply the mixed glaze evenly to the surface using the appropriate-size brush. Finish by painting in one direction only.

3 Wearing rubber gloves, remove the rag and wring it out. Be careful to catch any excess glaze in the tub and to work any excess solution from your gloves back into the rag.

4 Scrunch the rag into a sausage shape about 4 inches long. Don't try to fold it; this would give you the wrong paint effect.

5 Apply the rag to the surface by gently rolling it up in a straight line, using both hands. When the first column is complete, overlap it slightly onto the second for a continuous, seamless finish.

6 It's easiest to complete walls in sections, taking the first section as high as you can comfortably reach and staggering the tops of the columns. A staggered top will make your joints easier to disguise.

7 As the rag becomes wetter, the finish on the wall will change. To prevent this, dab the rag on an absorbent cloth to wipe off excess glaze. Use a ragging technique (see pages 44–45) on tight areas and corners.

8 The result is ideal for a variety of surfaces, from door panels to walls and even some floors.

ALTERNATIVE EFFECTS

Stippling
Stippling over the base glaze (left) then rag-rolling creates a lightly textured effect (right).

Brushing
Brushing on the glaze randomly (left) then rag-rolling gives a crumpled effect (right).

THE MORE THE MERRIER

It's easier for two people to work together on large areas, one applying the glaze while the other does the ragging. Or, use a short-nap roller to cover large areas more quickly.

When making your test samples, use different types of fabrics for your rags. New fabrics always should be washed first since the texture they produce can change with use if they haven't been softened.

Stippling: one color

Stippling is a wonderful way to create shaded color that has no obvious direction or texture. It looks surprisingly natural and makes a subtle backdrop. Use soft base colors such as white, cream, and pastels and add stronger color glazes over them. Stippling also works with other finishes to soften textures that are too strong or to hide unsightly brush marks.

TOOLS: 1- to 3-inch paintbrush or short-nap roller (depending on size of area to be finished), stippling and edge-stippling brushes

MATERIALS: Drop cloth, 1 mixed glaze (see pages 54–55), old towel or absorbent cloth

BASE: This finish can be used over a good-condition, solid-colored surface painted with satin paint (see pages 36–37).

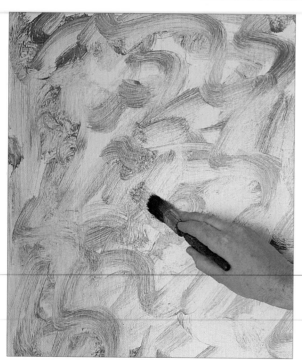

1 Using the appropriate-size paintbrush, apply the glaze randomly but evenly to the surface that you're stippling. Or, apply large areas of glaze using a short-nap paint roller.

2 Work a little glaze into the stippling brush to dampen it, then pound the surface, dabbing the brush evenly and firmly up and down, and keeping it perpendicular to the surface.

3 Control the density of the color by removing excess glaze from the brush as it builds up. Just dry the brush on a towel or absorbent cloth.

4 Continue to stipple the area, controlling the depth of color by repeating Step 3. Fix any mistakes immediately by stippling over them.

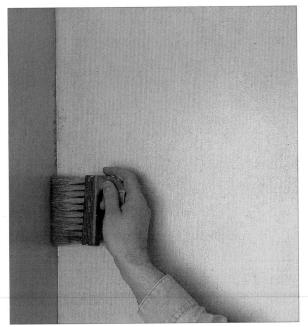

5 Use a narrow brush or edge stippler for a neat finish in awkward corners and against baseboards and door trim.

6 The final finish is a blend of background and glaze colors with no obvious brush marks, giving the surface a subtle, shaded look.

Stippling: two colors

By perfecting this finish and using it to blend two or more colors, you can create unusual shaded effects. For example, you can produce subtle color variations that seem to change the apparent shape of a room (see the large box on page 63). Then use a second color in a defined area, or subtly blend three areas of color into each other.

TOOLS: 1-inch paintbrush, stippling and edge-stippling brushes

MATERIALS: Drop cloth, mixed glazes in 2 or more colors (see pages 54–55), old towel or absorbent cloth

BASE: This finish can be used over a good-condition, solid-colored surface painted with satin paint (see pages 36–37).

2 Using a second brush, apply the second color in the same random way to the area you want to cover with this color.

1 Using the appropriate-size brush, apply the first glaze randomly but evenly over the entire area that you want to decorate with that color.

3 Work a little of the first glaze into the stippling brush to dampen it, and pound the glaze. Keep the brush perpendicular to the wall (see Step 2 on page 60).

4 When you've stippled the first color, roughly clean the stippling brush on the towel or use a second, clean brush to stipple the second color. It's inevitable—and desirable—that you'll blend the two colors.

5 Pound in the second color with the clean stippling brush until you're happy with the texture. It's easy to fix any mistakes as they happen—simply stipple over them.

6 Where colors meet, slowly blend the edges, merging the colors until you achieve the desired mix. You can control the density of color and texture by drying the brush often on the absorbent cloth.

7 Clean up corners and edges using a narrow brush or the narrow edge-stippler. You may need to dry the brush more frequently to remove excess glaze from the corners.

8 The result is a natural blend of colors that you can use effectively to add mottled color and texture to almost any surface, large or small.

THINK SMALL
Use a stencil brush to stipple small items.

TRICKS WITH COLOR
If you use one color, with a second color on center areas, the stippling will soften the edges and wall corners and give the impression of age.

Applying three shades of one color in lightly merging horizontal stripes—dark at the bottom and light at the top—makes the wall appear higher than it really is.

Bagging: one color

Bagging proves how easy paint finishing can be. There are few things more inexpensive and widely available than plastic bags, which, when crumpled up, produce swirling shapes and patterns in paint. You can experiment with this technique using other objects. Try a variety of simple household items to see what patterns and unusual decorative finishes they create.

TOOLS: 1-inch paintbrush, plastic bag

MATERIALS: Drop cloth, mixed glaze in 1 color (see pages 54–55), old towel or absorbent cloth

BASE: This finish can be used over a solid-colored surface painted with satin paint (see pages 36–37).

1 Using the appropriate-size brush, apply the glaze randomly but evenly to the surface.

2 Turn the plastic bag inside out, then crumple it into a shape that's comfortable to hold.

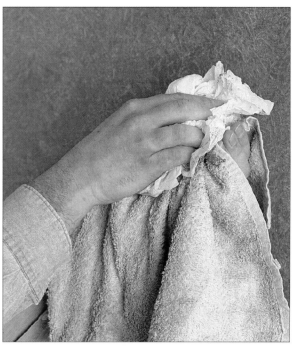

3 Gently pat the surface with the bag, reshaping it occasionally to create new patterns. Work quickly, paying special attention to corners and making the finish as even as possible.

4 You can remove glaze from the bag by occasionally drying it on a towel. Clean it more often if you're trying to achieve a finer texture and a softer color.

5 The finished pattern will appear dappled and grainy—like an exotic polished stone. It's important to keep the glaze wet while working on it, but because this is such a fast technique, even large areas can be covered by one person.

PLASTIC BAGS
Experiment with different kinds and thicknesses of bags to create a variety of textures. Before using any plastic bag, however, turn it inside out; if there happens to be any print on the outside, the glaze could dissolve it and it could end up smudging your work.

Bagging: two colors

Two-color bagging is a remarkably easy way to blend two colors to create a fascinating texture. Although it's certainly effective on its own, two-color bagging also provides the ideal background for marbling (see pages 86–87). It's quick to do and couldn't be easier or cheaper.

TOOLS: Two 1-inch paintbrushes, plastic bags

MATERIALS: Drop cloth, mixed glazes in 2 colors (see pages 54–55), old towel or absorbent cloth

BASE: This finish can be used over a solid-colored surface painted with satin paint (see pages 36–37). It's effective on walls, furniture, and woodwork, from door panels to tabletops.

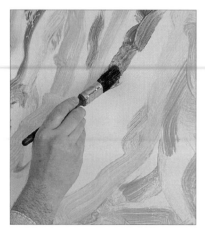

2 Turn your bag inside out and crumple it into a convenient shape. Bag size, thickness, and the way it's held all affect the final finish.

1 Using two paintbrushes, one for each color, apply both glazes randomly but evenly over the same area of surface but not on top of each other. To achieve a marbled effect, as shown here, work over a pale ivory base coat. The main glaze is a medium yellow; smaller areas of darker brown glaze—sparingly applied— are used to subtly suggest the strands, fissures, and other natural features of real stone.

3 Dab the bag over the surface (see Step 3 on page 65), applying it to one color first. Continue dabbing the area until you achieve a reasonable texture.

4 Clean the bag with the towel to get it ready for applying the second color areas. Or, simply replace the bag with a new one.

5 Dab the bag over the second color (repeating Step 3, opposite). Some overlap and mixing of color is inevitable and desirable at this stage.

WHIMSICAL MARBLE
Use this technique to create a whimsical marbled effect on hall walls or in a dining room on the area below a chair rail.

6 Carefully blend the colors by working from one glaze to the other. Continue until you achieve a look you're happy with. You can remove the glaze and change the texture by drying the bag with the towel.

7 The blended and textured finish is both quick and easy to achieve. Although its intriguing appearance might make it seem difficult to produce, in fact, it's just the opposite.

Color washing

A color wash made with glaze creates a layer of color through which the background color can still be seen. You can achieve a variety of effects using a brush or sponge. A brush gives a bolder, uneven finish in which streaks appear and the base color shows through more strongly in some places than others. A sponge creates a subtle haze. Make samples of several effects to help you decide on the best one for your room.

Using brushes
TOOLS: 1-inch paintbrush or short-nap roller, dragging brush or flogger

MATERIALS: Drop cloth, mixed glaze in 1 color (see pages 54–55), old towel or absorbent cloth

Using a sponge
TOOLS: Synthetic sponge

MATERIALS: Drop cloth, mixed glaze in 1 color (see pages 54–55), old plate, absorbent cloth or old towel

BASE: This finish can be used over a solid-colored surface painted with satin paint (see pages 36–37).

USING BRUSHES

1 Apply the glaze randomly but evenly to the surface using the appropriate-size brush. Since it's important to maintain a wet working edge, on large areas, you may need to work with a helper. Or, use a short-nap roller to apply the glaze more quickly.

2 Use a dragging brush dampened in the glaze to make short, random strokes, building up the pattern you've chosen. On larger areas, you may need to use a wider flogging brush. Dry the brush with a towel to remove excess glaze and to create a more subtle color.

3 The result is a three-dimensional, luminous finish that's equally suited to walls, floors, furniture, and even china. You can add more colors if you like—just let the previous coat dry completely before you add the next one.

USING A SPONGE

1 Prepare a protected work surface and round up all of your supplies. Pour a little glaze onto the plate and mop it up with the synthetic sponge. Work the sponge around the plate and make sure that the glaze is evenly distributed on the sponge.

2 Use the sponge to spread the glaze over the surface in a random, swirling motion. Reapply glaze to the sponge whenever it becomes necessary.

3 The result is a distinctive and very individual effect. You can enhance it by applying additional layers of color after the first coat has completely dried.

TWO-COLOR VARIATIONS

Swirls
Swirls, using two colors of a similar tone, create this delicate effect. Allow the first coat to dry completely, then repeat the process with the second color.

Swiping
Swiping the surface with widely sweeping brush strokes, first in one color and then in a second when the first is dry, creates a bolder and more uneven texture.

BRUSH EFFECTS
Random, overlapping brush strokes slowly build up over the surface, producing the effect shown on page 69, but you can create a checkerboard, plaid, or "hay bundle" finish, too.

SPONGE EFFECTS
Random, circular, and sweeping strokes made with a sponge give a cloudlike appearance.

Color rubbing

This is a technique that highlights the patterns in an embossed surface.

A glaze in a darker color is applied over a light-colored base. The raised areas of the design are rubbed to expose the base color, letting the top coat of glaze appear more strongly on the raised areas. This emphasizes the three-dimensional nature of the surface. Always test a small area first; rubbing can expose the seams on some embossed wallpaper.

Embossed wall coverings
TOOLS: 2-inch paintbrush or short-nap roller, rubber-bladed window-cleaning squeegee

MATERIALS: Drop cloth, mixed glaze in 1 color (see pages 54–55), old towel

Plaster and carvings
TOOLS: Two 2-inch paintbrushes, rubber-bladed window-cleaning squeegee

MATERIALS: Drop cloth, mixed glazes in 2 colors (see pages 54–55), absorbent, lint-free cloth

BASE: Use satin paint (see pages 36–37).

EMBOSSED WALL COVERINGS

1 Use darker glazes over a light-colored semigloss paint base (see pages 36–37).

2 Apply the glaze evenly to the embossed surface using a brush or short-nap roller.

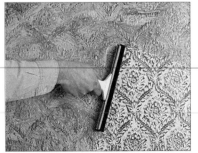

3 Gently wipe the surface with the squeegee, working in all directions to ensure a completely even finish.

4 Remove excess glaze from the squeegee with a towel whenever it builds up. Continue working the entire surface.

5 The result is a buildup of glaze in the crevices with little on the highest areas, highlighting the embossed design.

PLASTER AND CARVINGS

1 Apply two colors of glaze randomly but evenly to the surface using the appropriate-size brushes. Here, blue and brown blend to produce an "aged" effect.

2 Move the brush in an up-and-down stippling motion (see pages 62–63) until the colors partially blend.

3 Form a pad from the absorbent, lint-free cloth, and wipe it carefully over the surface. Turn and refold the cloth when it becomes covered with glaze to keep it uniformly clean.

4 The result has the look of a patina produced by age, with an appealing blend of colors. For an even richer, more antiqued effect, additional color or a crackle finish (see pages 80–81) can be added after this base is completely dry.

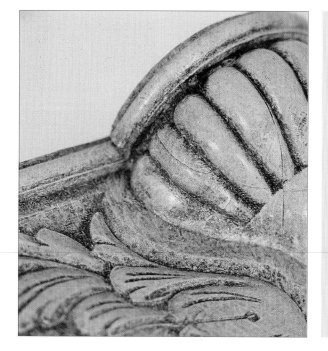

VARIATIONS

For large areas of shallow moldings, a short-nap roller also would work to apply the glaze in Step 1.

A ragged texture can be achieved by using a crumpled rag to dab the surface when Step 3 is completed. Experiment by trying a variety of common household items as applicators.

Combing

Combing originally was designed to give a simple wood-grain effect. In fact, it's much more versatile than this. Combs are used to create a wide variety of patterns, from simple trellis or cane effects to wild or delicate three-dimensional moiré patterns, and even impressive plaids.

TOOLS: 1-inch paintbrush or short-nap roller, stippling brush, comb

MATERIALS: Drop cloth, mixed glaze in 1 color (see pages 54–55), old towel or absorbent cloth

BASE: This finish can be used over a solid-colored surface painted with satin paint (see pages 36–37)

1 Apply the glaze evenly to the surface using the paintbrush. To cover large areas quickly, use a short-nap roller. Better yet, make it easy on yourself and enlist a friend to help you apply the finish.

2 Stipple the surface (see pages 60–61) to remove brush strokes and ensure the even distribution of the glaze. When necessary, use a towel to wipe excess glaze from the brush.

3 Hold the comb at about a 30-degree angle to the surface, and draw it through the glaze. Achieve different finishes by varying the pressure and the angle of the comb.

4 Remove excess glaze often by cleaning the comb with the towel. If you're not happy with the finish, repeat steps 2–4.

COMBING PATTERNS

Moiré
Straight, overlapping, slanted lines combine to create a moiré effect.

Basket
A simple basketweave pattern looks good on panels surrounded by a dragged frame (see pages 56–57).

Swirls
Try your hand at freehand drawing by using a comb like a calligraphy pen.

Music
The design shown here would appeal to a budding musician.

MAKE YOUR OWN COMBS
You can easily make your own combs by cutting slits in pieces of stiff cardboard or the blade of a rubber squeegee.

Antiquing and Faux Finishes

With time, the finish on old furniture and decorative items crazes, fades, and wears, and it's these signs of age that antiquing seeks to copy. Antiquing techniques take advantage of the interaction between incompatible materials to simulate the effects of age. Look carefully at old, worn surfaces to see where aging occurs naturally—usually on corners, edges, and around handles—then use this information to create a realistic copy.

You also can use paint effects to simulate expensive materials such as marble or to reproduce wood grains. These faux finishes are best used where the materials they copy would appear naturally in the home. Whenever possible, use a sample of the real thing as a guide for your colors and patterns.

Distressing

Distressing produces a worn, country look on new furniture and paneling. It's achieved by removing part of the top coat of paint to display a different color base, and by using metal objects like keys and chains to bruise the surface and simulate wear. Although water-based paint is used here, you also can create the finish with oil-based paints.

TOOLS: Steel wool, 2-inch paintbrushes, keys on a ring or metal chain, fine-grit sandpaper

MATERIALS: Water-based paints in 2 contrasting colors, petroleum jelly

BASE: This finish can be used over a natural-wood surface (see pages 36–37). Use it to decorate furniture, wall panels, baseboards, doors, and other woodwork.

1 Using a brush and the color that will show through the distressed areas, paint on the base coat. When it's dry, apply small smears of petroleum jelly with your thumb to the areas that you want to show through the top surface. Pay special attention to corners and edges.

2 Old furniture shows its age with the knocks and bruises it gets from everyday use. If you want to simulate them on a new piece of furniture, use a set of keys or a chain to beat the surface of the furniture, bruising it and making it look worn.

3 When you're happy with the worn effect that you've given the surface, apply the top coat of paint over the entire piece in the normal way, and let it dry thoroughly.

4 Take the steel wool, form it into a pad, and vigorously rub it over the surface. The top coat won't stick to the areas covered with the petroleum jelly, so the paint will be easy to remove.

5 If you need to soften the edges and remove additional paint, smooth the surface with fine-grit sandpaper to let more of the base color show through.

6 Over scratched surfaces covered with water-based paint, apply two or three coats of varnish, sanding lightly between coats to provide tooth for the next coat. This will protect the finish.

7 The result is a worn, two-color finish that blends perfectly with old furniture and antiques.

ADDING COLORS

If you like, you can add more than one color to simulate layers of paint that have built up over the years.

For additional highlights, rub a little gilding cream over the surface when you're completely finished with the layers and the paint has dried.

DECORATING TIPS

You can use a wax candle in place of petroleum jelly. Just rub the tip of the candle over the areas where you don't want the paint to adhere.

Water-based buttermilk or Shaker paints will produce the soft and subtle colors associated with age.

Choose colors that contrast, so one will show up against the other. Both colors should coordinate with your room's color scheme.

Wax aging

This effect takes advantage of the interaction between turpentine-based wax and water-based paint to produce an overall faded look. The finish is similar to—but a little more subtle than—the distressing shown on pages 76–77, where worn areas are clearly defined. The wax, applied with steel wool, softens the paint, making areas of the top coat easy to remove.

TOOLS: 1-inch paintbrush, medium to fine-grade steel wool

MATERIALS: Drop cloth, flat water-based paint in 2 contrasting colors, turpentine-based furniture wax, clean soft cloth

BASE: This finish is best for small or ornate objects such as picture frames, and turned wood such as banisters and towel rails, as shown here. Prepare the surface according to advice given on pages 36–37.

1 Protect your work surface with a drop cloth. Prepare the item to be finished (see pages 34–35), then apply one coat of flat water-based paint with a paintbrush. Let the paint dry.

2 When the first coat of paint is dry, apply the contrasting color paint. Let this coat of paint dry thoroughly.

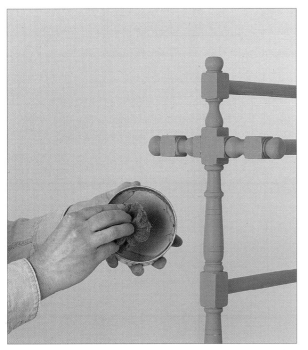

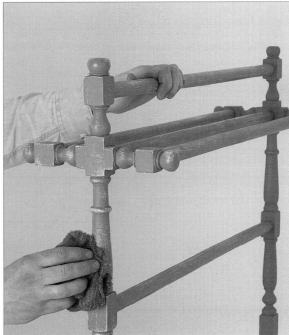

3 Fold the steel wool into a pad and work a little wax into it. Vigorously rub the pad over the entire surface.

4 Try to remove only part of the water-based top coat over the whole surface. Continue until you feel you've removed enough of the top coat, then let the wax harden.

5 When the wax is hard, buff it to a satin sheen using a soft cloth. You'll be amazed at how easy this aged finish is to produce and how convincing it is to look at.

SMALL IS BEAUTIFUL
Apply a small amount of artist's oil paint with the steel wool and wax (see Steps 3 and 4) to further beautify the finish.

Acrylic crackle finishes

Acrylic crackle glaze and varnish produce fascinating crazed surfaces that make new objects, such as shelves or boxes, look like old prized possessions. Crackle glaze works by splitting two layers of water-based paint so the first coat shows through the cracks. Crackle varnish creates a web of fine cracks over a base coat.

Acrylic crackle glaze
TOOLS: 1-inch paintbrush, fine-grade steel wool, fine-grit sandpaper

MATERIALS: Drop cloth, flat water-based or acrylic paint in 2 colors, acrylic crackle glaze, fine-grit sandpaper, flat acrylic varnish

Acrylic crackle varnish
TOOLS: See crackle glaze, left.

MATERIALS: Drop cloth, water-based or acrylic paint, crackle varnish and crackle glaze, clean, soft cloth, artist's oil paint, turpentine, flat acrylic varnish

BASE: Use over acrylic or water-based paints (see pages 34–35).

ACRYLIC CRACKLE GLAZE

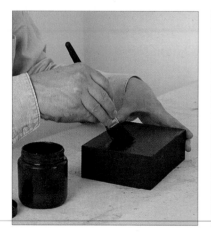

1 Protect your work surface with the drop cloth. Use a paintbrush to paint your chosen item with flat water-based or acrylic paint, using the color that you've chosen to show through the cracks.

2 After the base coat has thoroughly dried, apply an even coat of acrylic crackle glaze, brushing it on in one direction only. Apply the thickness that worked best for your test samples (see the Testing Crackle Glaze box opposite). Let it dry.

3 Next, apply the top coat, using a well-loaded brush and steady strokes, and working in the same direction as for the crackle glaze. Avoid going over the surface more than once with the brush; cracks will start to form immediately.

4 Let the surface dry. You'll find that cracks will continue to form as the top coat dries, revealing the base-paint color beneath.

5 When the piece is dry, sand it lightly and brush on one coat of flat acrylic varnish to protect the finish.

ACRYLIC CRACKLE VARNISH

1 Apply a base coat of water-based or acrylic paint in your chosen color. When it's completely dry, use a paintbrush to apply a sealing mixture of crackle glaze and crackle varnish, mixed in equal proportions.

2 When this sealer layer has thoroughly dried, apply an even but thin layer of acrylic crackle varnish, brushing it on in one direction only. As this thin layer dries, it will shrink to create a web of fine surface cracks.

4 Let the piece dry, then varnish it for protection.

HIGHLIGHTING
With crackle glaze, colors of similar intensity produce the best results. Try using gilding cream in place of artist's oils to add glitter to the cracks.

3 To highlight the cracks after the varnish has dried, use a soft cloth to rub a small amount of artist's oil paint over the surface. Remove any excess paint with a cloth that's been dampened in thinner or turpentine.

TESTING CRACKLE GLAZE
The thickness of the coat of glaze determines the final result—the thicker the glaze, the more pronounced the crackling will be. So always make test samples to be sure that the final finish will turn out as expected.

Craquelure

Craquelure creates a more delicate crazed effect than the crackle finishes shown on pages 80–81, so it's best to use on fine finishes such as decoupage, stenciling, and hand painting. The craquelure finish is transparent and gives just a slight suggestion of age.

TOOLS: 1-inch paintbrushes, hair dryer

MATERIALS: Drop cloth, acrylic or oil-based varnish (Step 1), patina varnish, cracking varnish, artist's oil paints, soft rags, thinner or turpentine, oil-based varnish (Step 5)

BASE: Use craquelure to age delicate finishes such as decoupage, stenciling, and hand painting. Prepare the surface as described in Step 1 below.

 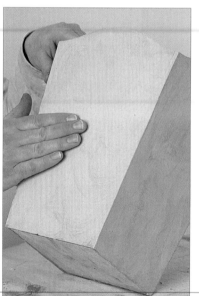 

1 Protect the work surface with a drop cloth. Brush acrylic- or oil-based varnish over the previously painted surface to seal it completely. Allow it to dry thoroughly. When it's dry, apply a coat of patina varnish as evenly as you can.

2 Humidity, air circulation, and temperature will affect the drying rate, but the surface should be left only until it's tacky or just dry to the touch. As a general rule, the drier the base coat, the finer the resulting cracks will be.

3 As soon as the surface is ready, apply an even coat of gum arabic (cracking varnish) over the base coat. If the cracking varnish starts to split and separate, mix in a little household detergent to reverse the process. Let it dry.

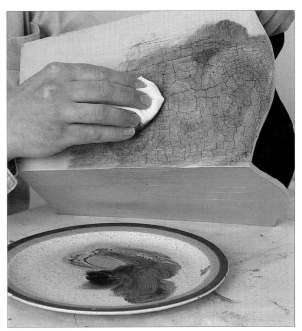

4 Use a hair dryer set on low heat to speed the drying process. Fast drying tends to create larger cracks than you'd get otherwise.

5 When the surface is completely dry, highlight the cracks by rubbing artist's oil paint into them with a soft rag. Remove any excess paint with a little thinner or turpentine. When the artist's oil paint is dry, protect the surface by applying a layer of oil-based varnish.

6 The result is a crazed finish that looks surprisingly natural. You can enhance both plain and painted surfaces with this technique.

SURFACE HIGHLIGHTS

Never use water-based highlighting media; they'll soften the cracking varnish. If you want to give the surface a metallic gleam, rub gilding cream into the cracks.

Liming

Traditional liming goes back to the 16th century, when lime was used to keep woodworm at bay. Today, this lethal material has been largely replaced with a much safer product that adds the same white gleam and highlights the grain of the wood.

TOOLS: Stiff wire brush, fine-grade steel wool

MATERIALS: Drop cloth, liming paste, furniture wax, soft cloth or brush

BASE: Stripped or bare wood is the best base. For painted or varnished wood, prepare the surface by thoroughly stripping it with a commercial stripper.

2 Using fine-grade steel wool, work a little liming paste into the surface of the wood, rubbing in all directions to cover the area completely.

1 Protect the work surface with a drop cloth. Brush the stripped or bare wood surface vigorously with the stiff wire brush to remove the soft grain and roughen the surface.

3 Leave the item in a cool place until the paste is almost dry as per the manufacturer's directions. Then work a small amount of furniture wax into a clean ball of steel wool.

4 Rub the wax over the limed surface in a circular motion. Turn the steel wool frequently and apply more wax whenever necessary.

5 When you've achieved the desired finish, let it dry for about 30 minutes, then buff it to a satin finish with a soft cloth or brush.

6 The liming paste adds a traditional white sheen to the clearly defined surface grain.

CAUTION
Always read the manufacturer's instructions and safety precautions carefully whenever you're using paint stripper.

IT'S A WHITEWASH
For a good alternative to liming, apply a whitewash (see pages 48–49) to untreated bare wood, then rub it with steel wool. Wax when it's dry.

Basic marbling

Marbling is an art form in its own right, but without a whole lot of effort, you still get acceptable results. You'll achieve a more realistic effect if you use a slab of real marble or a photograph of marble as a reference. Here especially, it's best to start with a small piece, such as a shelf or table.

TOOLS: Plastic bags, old plate, natural sea sponge, feathers, fine artist's brush, softening brush, stippling brush

MATERIALS: Glazes in 2 or more colors, mineral spirits or turpentine, artist's oil paint

BASE: This finish can be used over a solid-colored surface painted with satin paint (see pages 36–37). Marbling is ideal for items that might naturally be made of marble, such as tabletops, shelves, and lamp bases.

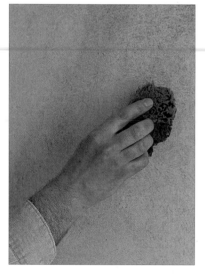

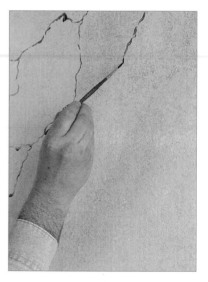

1 Use the bagging technique (see pages 66–67) to blend two or more colored glazes on the surface. Pour a small amount of mineral spirits or turpentine onto an old plate. Mop it up with a natural sea sponge, and lightly dab it over the glazed surface.

2 After a minute or so, the surface will break up into small, fossil-like patterns. If the patterns don't appear, then the glaze was too dry; in that case, remove the glaze using a lint-free cloth and solvent, and start again. Remove excess solvent before proceeding by lightly stippling the surface or dabbing it with a soft, absorbent cloth.

3 Use artist's oils thinned with a little solvent or glaze mixture to paint veins. A fine artist's brush will work, but experiment with other fine brushes, too. Try to achieve a real-looking vein; refer often to the pattern of veins on your sample slab or photograph.

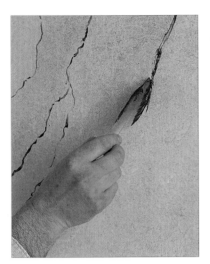 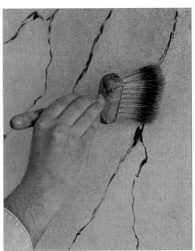 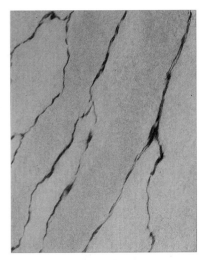

4 You can use the edge of a feather, close to the tip, to create a natural vein effect, but you'll need to practice the technique. All veins should run in the same direction and continue over the edges of the surface. Don't add too many veins.

5 Use a softening brush to blur the hard lines of the veins. Apply the brush with very light arcing strokes. First work in the direction of the veins and then at a right angle to them. If brush strokes appear, you're applying too much pressure; ease up a bit for a more natural effect.

6 The result is a blended and textured background with marblelike veins running throughout. When the surface has dried completely, you can add more layers of glaze to enhance and enrich the final finish.

ALTERNATIVE METHOD

If you don't want to soften the background as shown in Step 5, you can let the bagged surface dry and apply the veins at a later time.

A clean dusting or dragging brush is a good alternative to a softening brush.

Additional layers of glaze and veining will enhance the finish and create the depth of color and texture found in natural marble.

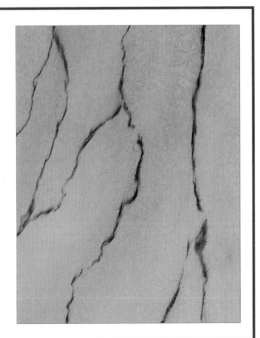

THE SPATTER TECHNIQUE

If you like, you can spatter mineral spirits over the wet, glazed surface using a short-bristled brush, such as a stencil brush. Just tap the shaft of the brush on a ruler or the side of your hand to send tiny specks of mineral spirits onto the marbled surface.

Marbling a large area

Most natural stone, including marble, is cut and used as slabs. So if you want large areas of marbling to look authentic, you need to break them down into smaller blocks for painting. You can lay out your slab shapes to resemble individual blocks or even intricate mosaic patterns. But, again, careful planning is essential. Draw a layout to scale, mark all of the slabs on it, then use your plan to draw the design on the actual surface. Realistic patterns and shapes will not only enhance the final effect but also will make your painting easier.

TOOLS: Steel rule, straightedge, pencil or chalk, masking tape, lining pen

BASE: This finish can be used over a solid-colored surface painted with satin paint (see pages 36–37). It is ideal on floors, walls, and work surfaces.

PLANNING LARGE AREAS

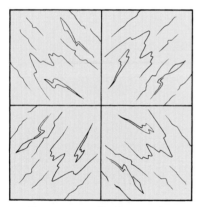

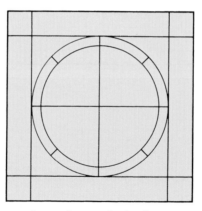

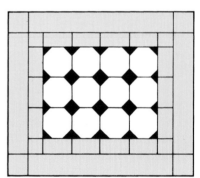

1 For an overall whimsical effect, let the marbling cover a large continuous area. For a realistic effect, you'll need to create the appearance of individual slabs. The pattern should radiate from a central point and consist of slabs that are mirror images of each other.

2 Areas also can be broken into more complex arrangements. You'll need to measure the area carefully and draw a plan to scale. Then work out your design on the plan.

3 When you're happy with the design, transfer it to the area to be marbled. Use a steel rule to measure distances accurately, then use chalk or a soft pencil and a straightedge to carefully lay out the design.

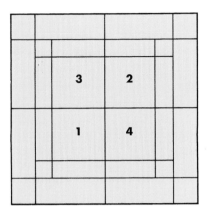

4 You'll need to allow one slab area to dry before working on those next to it. Plan a work order, and number your squares to avoid problems. Use masking tape to protect adjacent areas while you work, then move on to an area that doesn't border the wet slab. Allow sufficient drying time before starting work on shapes that are next to the ones you've just painted.

5 Whimsical marbling covers large areas. But for a more realistic look, use a soft pencil and straightedge to mark joints between blocks or slabs. Finally, varnish the surface to protect it. This is especially important in areas such as halls and stairways, which get hard wear.

SOFTENED EFFECTS

Marbling techniques in soft shades used in an impressionistic manner create a restful look that's easy to live with. Not only are such effects ideal for rough, damaged walls, but they also lend a rich look of age to a new home.

GETTING VEINS RIGHT

Take your time when creating the veining, and work on only one panel at a time. In real marble, veins are never parallel, wobbly, or cobweb-patterned. Although they don't break, they may split and form junctions.

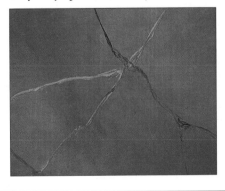

Wood graining

Wood graining imitates natural wood or creates wood patterns in decidedly unnatural colors. Plywood and medium-density fiberboard (MDF) are easy to enhance with the look of expensive hardwoods. Here, a comb is used for one finish and a rocker for the other. (The rocker has a curved and embossed face and is used in a gentle rocking motion, changing the angle of the face.) As always, practice with samples to perfect your technique before working on the actual surface.

Using a comb
TOOLS: 1-inch paintbrush, softening brush, comb (metal or rubber)

MATERIALS: Drop cloth, mixed glaze in 1 color (see pages 54–55), absorbent cloth

BASE: This finish can be used over a solid-colored surface painted with satin paint (see pages 36–37).

Using a rocker
TOOLS: 1-inch paintbrush, straightedge, rocker

MATERIALS: Drop cloth, mixed glaze in 1 color (see pages 54–55), varnish, absorbent cloth

BASE: This finish can be used over a solid-colored surface painted with satin paint (see pages 36–37).

USING A COMB

1 Brush on the glaze in random arcs. Then repeatedly pull the comb through the glaze, cleaning it on the cloth after each stroke.

2 Use a softening brush and steady, light strokes to feather and soften hard edges.

3 Wrap an absorbent rag around your finger and wipe through the glaze in random arcs. Then comb through the glaze.

4 Use the softening brush to blur hard edges until you achieve the desired effect. Protect the surface with varnish when it's dry.

USING A ROCKER

1 Apply the glaze evenly to the surface using a paintbrush. Follow the direction of the grain with your brush strokes.

2 To simulate boards, place a straightedge against the surface. Steadily draw the rocker through the glaze, guiding it with the straightedge and gently rocking it back and forth.

3 Move the straightedge over and position it parallel to the previous line, forming a gap that's slightly larger than the width of the rocker. Continue by repeating Step 2.

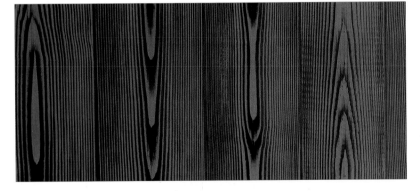

4 The result is a realistic and easy-to-achieve pine wood grain. When the glaze is dry, varnish the surface to protect and beautify it.

COLORFUL EFFECTS
Don't be afraid to use bright colors for this finish. These examples show the effect of using strong colors and overlapping the strokes of the rocker.

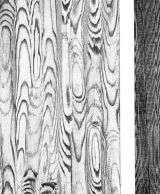 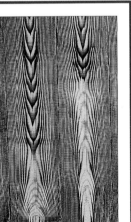

SMOOTH ROCKING
Pretinted oil glazes in assorted wood-tone colors are available from specialty retailers. Wipe some silicon lubricant onto the straightedge to help smooth out the rocking process.

Glossary

Acrylic
A fast-drying water-based material with a tough, waterproof finish.

Aging
The process of simulating the effects of natural wear.

Artist's oils
An oil-based pigment used to tint transparent oil glaze.

Badger brush
A high-quality, expensive softening brush used with advanced glaze finishes (see page 20 for alternatives).

Bagging
A paint finish created using plastic bags.

Beeswax
A high-quality wax polish.

Cissing
Spattering on a paint solvent to "age" a finish by causing the top layer of paint to split.

Color rubbing
Using a cloth to remove glaze from certain areas.

Color washing
A subtle color effect created with sponges or brushes.

Complementary colors
Boldly contrasting colors from opposite sides of the color wheel.

Crackle glaze
A medium that causes splitting or cracking when used between two layers of water-based paint.

Craquelure
Fine-quality crazing created by using two varnishes that work against each other.

Distressing
Imitating wear and tear on painted surfaces (see Aging).

Dragging
Creating a contrasting lined effect using glaze.

Flogger
A long mixed-bristle brush for wood graining or dragging.

Glaze
A transparent medium that can be tinted any color and used for paint effects.

Graining
A technique that uses glazes to imitate wood grain.

Liming
Adding a white highlight and finish to open-grain wood.

Linseed oil
The base for traditional oil-based paints and transparent oil glazes.

Marbling
A technique that produces the look of stone.

Melamine
A plastic spray coating that can be painted or finished.

Pigment
A natural color source.

Primary colors
Yellow, blue, and red, from which all other colors can be mixed.

Ragging
Using a rag to create a decorative paint effect.

Rocker
A tool used to produce an effect that imitates wood grain.

Sandpaper
An abrasive used to remove roughness and smooth surfaces.

Satin
A durable paint that's a good base for most glaze finishes.

Softener
A brush for smoothing and toning to create a natural look.

Solvent
A cleaning or thinning agent for paints and finishes.

Universal stains
A pigment-based medium used to tint paints and glazes.

Varnish
A protective coating that may be water- or oil-based.

Water-based glaze
A water-based latex that forms a clear protective seal for the paint finish.

Index

Meredith® Press
An imprint of Meredith® Books

Do-It-Yourself Decorating
Step-by-Step Decorative Painting
Editor, Shelter Books: Denise L. Caringer
Contributing Editor: David A. Kirchner
Contributing Designer: Jeff Harrison
Copy Chief: Angela K. Renkoski

Meredith® Books
Editor in Chief: James D. Blume
Managing Editor: Christopher Cavanaugh
Director, New Product Development: Ray Wolf
Vice President, Retail Sales: Jamie L. Martin

Meredith Publishing Group
President, Publishing Group: Christopher M. Little
Vice President and Publishing Director: John P. Loughlin

Meredith Corporation
Chairman of the Board and Chief Executive Officer: Jack D. Rehm
President and Chief Operating Officer: William T. Kerr
Chairman of the Executive Committee: E. T. Meredith III

First published 1996 by Haynes Publishing

All of us at Meredith® Books are dedicated to providing you with information and ideas you need to enhance your home. We welcome your comments and suggestions about this book on stenciling. Write to us at: Meredith® Books, Do-It-Yourself Editorial Department, RW-206, 1716 Locust St., Des Moines, IA 50309-3023.

This edition published by Meredith Corporation, Des Moines Iowa, 1997
Printed in France
Printing Number and Year: 5 4 3 2   00 99 98
Library of Congress Catalog Card Number: 96-78040
ISBN: 0-696-20678-1